ROMANICHAL
GYPSIES

Thomas Acton and David Gallant

WAYLAND

Other titles in the Threatened Cultures series

Australian Aborigines   *Maori*
Bedouin   *Native Americans*
Inuits   *Rainforest Amerindians*
Kalahari Bushmen   *Saami of Lapland*
Kurds   *Tibetans*

Series editor: Paul Mason
Project editor: Katie Orchard
Design: Kudos Editorial and Design Services

Cover: Anita Bowers, a Romanichal Gypsy.
The cover border was painted by Delaine LeBas (see page 40).
Title page: Mrs Wood, a Kali Gypsy from North Wales.

Acknowledgements:
The authors wish to thank the many Gypsies and others who helped in the preparation of this book, especially Bubbles Brazil, Sylvia Dunn, Eli Frankham, Ian Hancock, Val and Percy Harris, Fay Williams, Delaine LeBas, Tom Lee, Peter Mercer, Charlie Smith and Maxine Turner. Thanks also to Kodak Ltd and the University of Greenwich for their generosity and support throughout this project. The authors are grateful for special permission to reproduce the poem by Charlie Smith on page 29. Poetry books by Charlie Smith are available from G.C.E.C.W.C.R., 8 Hall Road, Aveley, Essex RM15 4HD.

All the photographs in this book were taken by David Gallant.

None of the names in this book are fictitious. All of us are proud of who we are.

First published in 1997 by
Wayland Publishers Limited
61 Western Road, Hove
East Sussex BN3 1JD, England

British Library Cataloguing in Publication Data
Acton, T.
　Romanichal Gypsies.– (Threatened Cultures)
　1. Gypsies – Juvenile literature
　I. Title II. Gallant, D.
　305.8'91497

ISBN 0 7502 1260 8

Typeset by Malcolm Walker of Kudos Design, England
Printed and bound by L.E.G.O. S.p.A., Italy

Contents

A Gypsy family

Jimmy Harris was two when the picture below was taken. He lives with his mum, dad and two brothers on the Thistlebrook Gypsy caravan site in the London Borough of Greenwich. The site was built twenty years before Jimmy was born. The borough forced Gypsies, or Romanichals as they call themselves, to sell land they had owned for a long time, so it could become a council site.

Jimmy and his brothers, Danny and Sam, live in a caravan, or trailer, which has a kitchen at one end near the entrance, a living area, and a bedroom at the other end. Jimmy's dad, Percy, bought the trailer from another Gypsy. Jimmy's grandparents, Laily and Joseph Harris, also live on the Thistlebrook site and often come to visit.

There are usually no toilets or showers in trailers because Romanichals think this is dirty, or *mochadi*. In the days of horse-drawn wagons Gypsies used to make latrines in the countryside, well away from their camps. Today, most councils provide each family on their site with a utility block with toilets, showers, sinks and electricity. At Thistlebrook, the utility blocks were rebuilt after these photographs were taken. Jimmy's mother, Val, does the laundry in hers.

◄ *Jimmy Harris plays with a wheel, a symbol of 1,000 years of Romany travelling.*

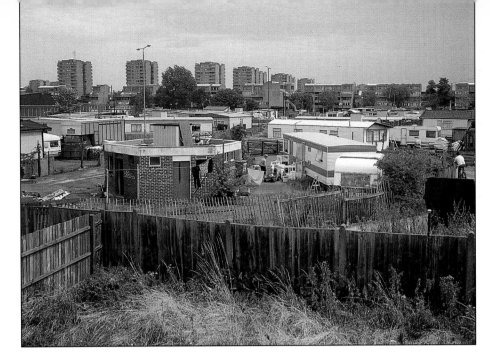

Double-unit trailers sometimes have a bathroom, separated from the living-space by a double wall.

While his older brothers, and his cousins are at school, Jim plays on the site. He is also learning, watching his mother tidying the trailer, and watching the men sorting scrap metal and mending their cars and pick-up trucks. Jimmy sometimes has a go at mending trucks himself. In the picture on page 4, Jimmy is holding a wheel from a bicycle, which is called *prastering saster* (meaning 'running iron') in English Romany.

Gypsies brought the Romany language with them when they left India about 1,000 years ago. Different Romany groups live in many countries. When some of these groups came together in 1971 to form the World Romany Congress, they put a wheel on their flag as a symbol of their long travels. Jimmy's wheel looks like the wheel on the Gypsy flag, and reminds us of all the wheels that have taken the Romany peoples from their original Indian homeland throughout the world over the past 1,000 years.

At Thistlebrook, the caravans stand on concrete pitches, with spaces outside for cars. When Gypsies owned the land there was space for seventy trailers and wagons. The Caravan Sites Act of 1968 said that councils had to build more sites for Gypsies. But when the council took over this land they cut the number to fifty-four pitches, and now there are fewer than fifty. Only a few families who have been on the site a long time are now allowed to keep lorries, or horses in stables, for which they are charged extra rent. Many Gypsies born in the borough cannot find a place to stop on the site.

Gypsies can be thrown off the site without a reason being given. This happened to one elderly couple, Mr and Mrs Powell. They tried to take the council to the European Court of Human Rights to say they should have the same rights as ordinary council tenants, but failed. Nevertheless, Gypsy families at Thistlebrook use the same shops, schools and facilities as other local people. Even postmen and dustmen now visit the site. Some familes on the site are well-off and have planted gardens around their smart mobile homes. Others have older trailers, but all of them try to have their own style. Many people now believe it would have been better to leave the Gypsies as owners of the land and help them develop it themselves.

Family connections are very important on Thistlebrook. As he grows up, Jimmy's relations will not just be the foundation of his social life, but also the people who will teach him how to earn a living and with whom he does business. The Harris family have travelled round Kent and London for generations. His mother's family, the Frankhams, are even more widely travelled, and are famous for the professional boxers they have produced. One relation, Johnny Frankham, was the light-heavyweight boxing champion of England in the early 1980s.

One of Jimmy's grandmothers often drives down from Cambridgeshire to see them. But when she visits she often has business to do as well.

The Gypsies at Thistlebrook do various kinds of work. Many of the men call themselves 'general dealers'. Jimmy's dad, Percy, will turn his hand to anything. As in all communities, some Gypsies are rich, some are poor, and most are somewhere in between. They collect scrap metal and other materials that can be recycled, which they then sort out and sell to large scrapyards. Sometimes, Gypsies also buy and sell cars, trucks and horses. Many of the women on the site keep up their earning skills by flower-selling, so that they will have some work to fall back on. But the recession of the 1990s has made all these businesses difficult and some people need help from social security.

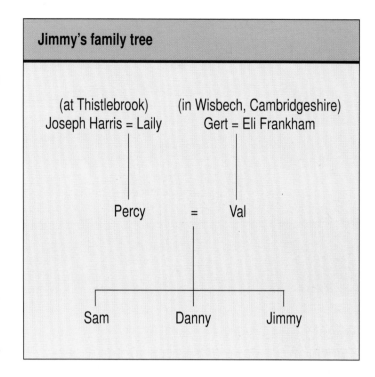

Jimmy's family tree

(at Thistlebrook)
Joseph Harris = Laily

(in Wisbech, Cambridgeshire)
Gert = Eli Frankham

Percy = Val

Sam   Danny   Jimmy

◄ *One of Jimmy's grandmothers, Gert Frankham, has driven her lorry from Wisbech, in Cambridgeshire, to visit the family in Thistlebrook. She will also try and sell some bulbs at the same time.*

▲ *While their grandmother is trying to 'have a deal', the Harris boys are playing with their friends. Behind them someone has brought in a wrecked Ford Capri to break up for scrap.*

Romanichals have faced such economic bad times before. When they first came to England around the year 1500, they were able to trade and put on shows for the nobility freely. But then unemployment hit the countryside. As merchants and townsfolk grew rich from the wool trade, agricultural workers were thrown out of work and wandered the country looking for work and food. Settled people became suspicious of vagrants. People also blamed foreigners for inflation and unemployment, and there were campaigns to send Gypsies, Jews and black people out of the country. By 1600, it was a crime punishable by death even to be an 'Egyptian' as the English, mistakenly, called Gypsies.

Sometimes, the local and Romanichal travelling craftspeople joined forces together and survived. It took them a long time to rebuild their lives, under the protection of big landowners who valued their services. But by the 1830s, Gypsies were again a thriving community and began to move from the tents they had lived in before to their new wooden living wagons, or *vardos*. They earned a good living from their trade with farmers.

◄ *Gypsy children on their way to school. Jimmy's Aunt Cindy and two other mothers from Thistlebrook walk the children to school past a corner of the site. Note the horse transporter and stables at the back on the right. Even on London sites, some Gypsies still keep and deal in horses.*

Then in the 1870s, cheap corn imported from the USA meant ruin for many English farmers and their Gypsy friends. Gypsies had to find trades in the towns, and many moved to the USA to keep their independance. Today, Gypsies have to balance their desire to be their own bosses, as their parents had been, with their eagerness to learn new skills.

Many teenage children still take time off school to learn their parents' trades. But secondary school attendance is better from Thistlebrook than from most Gypsy sites, because the site is so well-established. The schools have taken steps to respect the Gypsy way of life and make sure they meet Gypsy pupils' needs. Elsewhere, some Gypsy parents

► *Parents' evening: Sam's mother (left) discusses his schoolwork with his teacher. Boxgrove Primary School has taught Gypsy children, as well as other local children since it first opened. There are a lot of books about Romanichals and other Travellers on the school shelves. All children in the school are taught about the Romany contribution to life in Britain.*

▲ *One of Jimmy's cousins, Tracy (centre), with non-Gypsy friends in her class at Boxgrove School. This school encourages all children to be proud of themselves and their friends.*

see non-Gypsy children facing unemployment after they have left school and decide that their sons and daughters can do better out of school. Throughout Britain there are now more than 500 specialist teachers of Gypsy children, who visit Gypsy caravan sites to smooth the way for Gypsies into mainstream education. Many more teachers have Gypsy children in their classes.

Of course, some Gypsy children do well at school, and a small number go on to university or professional work. Going away to study is difficult. In a place such as Thistlebrook, local *gaujos* (non-Gypsies) know the Gypsies. At college, most people do not expect a fellow-student to be a Gypsy. Most people have never knowingly met a Gypsy, and many are very prejudiced. So it often seems easier for a Gypsy student to keep quiet about their background.

Many Gypsies living in houses do the same. Pretending to be *gaujos* means they do not have to face insults such as being called a 'Gyppo', but it makes them sad that they have to hide what they really are. But Gypsies in professional jobs sometimes find that joining Gypsy organizations, such as the Gypsy Council (see page 39), can give them the support and self-confidence to be proud of their Gypsy culture.

▲ *Jimmy's grandfather, Eli Frankham (right), at Appleby Fair — a traditional Gypsy gathering. Eli is sitting on the steps of a barrel-topped, horse-drawn wagon which belongs to his friend Gordon Boswell (centre). Gordon's father led the Gypsy campaign which saved the ancient fair at Appleby from closure in 1965. Gordon's great-grandfather helped write one of the first dictionaries of English Romany.*

One Gypsy who has started such an organization is Jimmy's grandfather, Eli Frankham. He has settled in a bungalow on his own land near Wisbech in Cambridgeshire and runs The National Romany Rights Association. In East Anglia, many shops and pubs refuse to serve the Gypsies who come to do summer work on farms, and councils try to stop Gypsies from getting planning permission to live in caravans on plots of land they buy. So there is plenty of work for the Romany Rights Association and other local groups.

At the moment, such politics do not interest Jimmy at all. Jimmy is much more interested in the hot weather. When the men come back from work and the children come back from school they are hungry (*bokkali* in Romany). The women cook for each person as he or she comes home; they don't all wait to eat together. Most men know how to cook too. And the ice-cream-van man knows he will find eager customers at about half-past four.

With his brothers and cousins around, Jimmy can play happily until it gets dark. Today, someone tries to teach him to ride a bicycle. After the hot, sticky weather of the day, Jimmy's brother helps him to wash his hair in the little yard, using the correct bowl so that the water runs down the drain by the utility block. Once his hair has dried, it is bedtime. Jimmy's mother washes his face and hands in another bowl inside the trailer.

Lollipops were probably a Romany invention. *Lolli* means 'red' and *pobbel* means 'apple'. In old fairground talk *cosh-lollipop* means a 'toffee apple'. *Cosh* is a Romany word for a stick, which has also been taken into English. *Lolli, pobbel* and *cosh* were all words brought by the Gypsies from India. Today, we still use the Romany word for a sweet snack on a stick that was used by the old Gypsy showmen who first sold them to children more than 200 years ago.

Jimmy's mother has stripped the walls of the trailer; but when the new wallpaper that he helped choose goes up, the walls will look really good. As Jimmy falls asleep he can hear his mum chatting over tea to his aunt in the living area. Outside the window he can hear his dad trying to bargain with a Traveller from Kent for a caged 'Goldfinch Mule' – a mixed breed of canary and goldfinch whose singing the Gypsies love. The last thing on Jimmy's mind is to hope that the weather tomorrow will be as good as it's been today.

▼ *The ice-cream-van. It is mid-afternoon, mid-July, 1994, and everyone wants an ice-cream. One of Jimmy's brothers has climbed on to the wheel to get a better view of the choice of ice-creams and lollipops.*

Romanichals and other Travellers

The Harris family call their own group of Gypsies Romanichals. The Romanichals originate from the mixture of Romany immigrants and local travelling craftspeople who survived the great persecutions of 1550–1650 in England. But today they live in

Romanichals in the USA

▲ *Danielle Morgan with her family on a small trailer site in Cedar Parks, near Austin, Texas, in the USA.*

In the nineteenth century, many English and European Gypsies moved to the USA. Today, there are probably over 100,000 Romanichals in the USA, more than in England. Like Romanichals in England, the Morgan family love to fill their trailer with beautiful china and decorations. Danielle's father, Dino, lays down asphalt on drives and yards for a living. This work is called 'blacktopping' in the USA and 'tarmacking' in England. Dino's roller is on the back of his white pick-up truck. Behind the truck is their trailer. The site is a small, private one, with only seven pitches on it, of which two are empty. Three of the pitches are occupied by non-Gypsy families in static mobile homes. In the USA, many people besides Gypsies live in caravans, so it is very easy to find places to stay, and caravan sites are much more spacious than in England.

▲ *Danielle Morgan in her trailer.*

several other countries, such as the USA and Australia, and other Gypsy groups have arrived, and are still coming, to England.

The Romany peoples who left India over 1,000 years ago were probably already made up of very different groups. They were linked by their ability to understand each others' North Indian dialects. These dialects fall into two big groups – the Eastern Gypsies, who call themselves Rom, and the Northern Gypsies who call themselves names such as Romanichals, Kalé and Sinti. There are about 8 million Eastern Gypsies and 2 million Northern Gypsies in the world today. Perhaps all the Northern groups originally called themselves Romanichals, but around 200 years ago, non-Gypsies began to use this word as an insult and it is no longer used in Europe, outside Britain.

The great persecutions of Gypsies worldwide, around 1600, left groups of Northern Gypsies stranded in various countries. Those who settled in England are the ancestors of today's Romanichals. They mix their Romany language with a lot of English which makes it hard for Gypsies from other groups in the world to understand them.

From 1850, when steamships and trains made international travel easier, Gypsies all round the world started moving on to different countries. Many English Gypsies went to the USA, Australia, New Zealand and South Africa. Some were forced to move to Australia by the British government as a punishment for being Gypsies.

Just as the Romanichals survived the persecutions of 1550–1650 in England, other Gypsy groups survived in the rest of Britain. In the Welsh-speaking areas of Wales, a small group calling themselves the Kalé, never more than 500 strong, kept themselves separate from the English, the Welsh and the Romanichals. They kept the Indian grammar and vocabulary of the Romany language.

Romany immigrants who reached Ireland, however, found a strong group of travelling traders already established, using a secret Celtic language called Shelta. Modern Irish Travellers are descended from a mixture of these groups. Today, they have the same cleanliness taboos against *mochadi* things as Romany people, and there is some Romany in their modern language, called Gammon.

◀ *Mrs Wood, a Kali Gypsy from North Wales, at Appleby Fair.*

▶ *Two Irish Minceir girls at Stow Fair in Gloucestershire. Behind them, a group of Romanichal and Minceir boys look at the ponies that have been brought for sale. Gypsies from all the groups in Britain go to the big fairs.*

◀ *A Romanichal family have brought their kid goats. Goats are just some of the animals that Gypsies like to keep.*

But Irish Travellers distinguish themselves strongly from Romanichals by saying 'We're not Gypsies, we're Irish Travellers'. By saying this they have sometimes been able to avoid the prejudice Gypsies have faced in Britain. In Europe, there are other small Gypsy groups, such as the Dutch Woonwagenbewoners and the Romanian Beash, who tried to escape being persecuted in the same way.

In their own language the Irish Travellers call themselves Minceir. There are about 25,000 Minceir in Britain and about 5,000 in the USA.

▲ *This boy's father is an Englishman who became fascinated by wooden wagons, married an Irish Traveller, and now lives with their young family on the road.*

In Scotland, a similar group call themselves the Scottish Travellers. Some of these Travellers also call themselves Gypsies, although others deny it! They call themselves Nawkens in their own language, Cant. Cant has three dialects (Highlands, Lowlands, and Borders) mixing Romany, Gaelic, Scots and Shelta in different proportions. There are about 20,000 Nawkens in Britain. About three-quarters of them live in houses. Traditionally, many travelled with tents or trailers only in the summer, and stayed in flats in Glasgow during the cold, Scottish winters.

The Kalé, Minceir, and Nawkens, together with 60,000 or so Romanichals, make up Britain's traditional Travellers. Nowadays, members of each group can be found on the roadside and at fairs throughout the whole of Britain. About half, in fact, live in houses, but still call themselves Travellers. Of course there are many inter-marriages, but each group's identity and language remain distinct. The Romanichals, however, make up more than half of the whole Traveller population in Britain. As well as their own dialects, other groups often speak English Romany, which is sometimes known as *pogadi jib*, (meaning 'broken tongue'), because of its mixture with English.

During the 1960s, some young English people who made their living from music festivals also began to live in trailers and old buses. They called themselves New Age Travellers. The housing crisis of the 1980s increased their numbers to more than 10,000.

The most successful New Age Travellers make their living from art or entertainment of various kinds, including small circuses they have created. They often buy old Gypsy caravans and try to learn about life on the road from Gypsies. But many New Age Travellers are poor, and dependent on social security. Often they find themselves in conflict with the law and the settled community, and with other Travellers who may see them as trouble-makers. Despite all these problems, they find this life preferable to the kind of accommodation into which homeless people are forced to live.

▲ *A New Age Traveller turns his hand to an old Gypsy craft, ironwork, with a mobile forge. Many New Age Travellers buy old trailers and equipment from Gypsies.*

Migration and travels

Gypsies are not always on the move. Most of the world's Gypsies live in houses in the same towns and villages in Eastern Europe that their ancestors lived in for generations. But Romany people have a reputation for travelling for two reasons:

a) The pull factor: some groups, such as the Romanichals, specialize in work that leads them to travel to different places. Such groups are called commercial nomads.

b) The push factor: Gypsies have often had to run away from persecution.

Bands of travelling metal workers, entertainers and soldiers, who had been on the losing side in wars, left India to become Romany peoples in Turkey and the Balkans about 1,000 years ago. They left behind Indian Gypsies, such as the Banjara, and passed by earlier emigrant commercial nomads (known as Nawar or Halebi) on the way. They brought with them Indian skills of metalworking, including the way to make gun metal.

In the sixteenth century, however, European countries began to become nation states. This meant that people began to believe each country should have only one kind of people living in it, and 'foreigners' should live in their own country. Many Jews, Gypsies and others who did not have their own country to go to were killed. Today, these ideas are called ethnic cleansing and people,

Romany refugees from Bosnia

There are about 500 Serbian Kalderash Rom refugees in London. Their ancestors were slaves in Romania, where slavery only ended in 1864. Then they moved to Yugoslavia. After 1950, some went to the West to work, returning with savings to build comfortable houses in Bosnia and Serbia. When war broke out, Muslims, Croats and Serbs each thought they belonged with one of the other groups. The refugees tell of being bombed and burned out, of Rom men conscripted into armies and forced to walk over minefields to test for safe paths with their lives. Militsa Djordjevic had 230 descendants in 1990. No one knows how many are still alive.

▶ *Militsa Djordjevic, (c1915–1995), a Serbian Kalderash Rom refugee in London.*

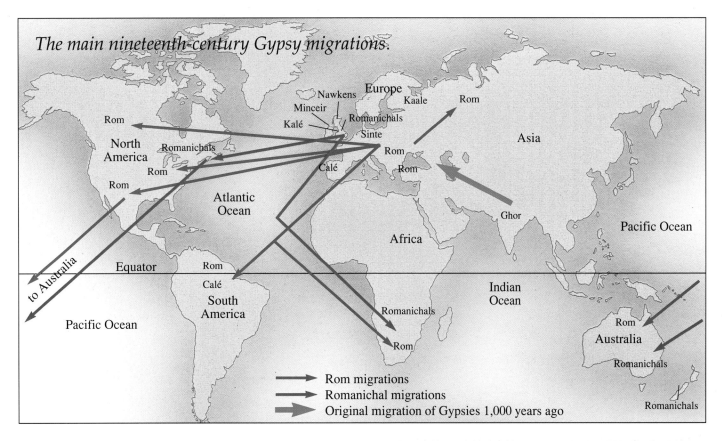

The main nineteenth-century Gypsy migrations.

Europe
Nawkens
Minceir
Kalé
Romanichals
Sinte
Kaale
Rom
Rom
North America
Romanichals
Rom
Rom
Calé
Rom
Rom
Asia
Ghor
Atlantic Ocean
Africa
Pacific Ocean
Equator
Rom
Calé
South America
Romanichals
Rom
Indian Ocean
to Australia
Pacific Ocean
Rom
Australia
Romanichals
Romanichals

→ Rom migrations
→ Romanichal migrations
→ Original migration of Gypsies 1,000 years ago

including Rom Gypsies, are still being killed in the former Yugoslavia, Romania and other countries. At least 100,000 have fled, mainly to Germany, Austria and Italy, but some also came to Britain.

The Dutch government in the eighteenth century, had a policy of getting rid of Gypsies. Some Gypsies tried to charter ships to escape to America, but they were chased by the Rotterdam port authorities who forced them to jump overboard. Nonetheless, a few reached Pennsylvania in the 1750s by selling themselves as slave labour. They escaped to form a community known as Chi-Keners or 'Black Dutch'. The few hundred Chi-Keners are the only Gypsies apart from English Gypsies who still call themselves Romanichals, since they escaped from Europe before the word Romanichal or Romanichel became a word of abuse. Today, many Chi-Keners have intermarried with English Gypsies in the USA.

▲ Francis Swartz, a 'Black Dutch' Romanichal in Texas, USA, sitting in front of his mobile home.

These Dutch and English Romanichals in the USA found they had very similar lifestyles. In England today, however, Romanichals realize that the Rom refugees from Eastern Europe have not only a different dialect of the Romany language, but also a very different way of life.

Many of the Rom, especially those who were settled until the 1850s in Romania, used to live in slave villages, where they had to sort out their own quarrels without involving their owners. They held their own courts,

▲ *Being moved on: sometimes Gypsies move because they want to, for reasons of business, family or pleasure. But sometimes the police give them no choice.*

called the *kris*. The Rom now hold *kris* all over Europe and America to settle important matters and will travel hundreds of miles to them.

Most Romanichals, however, believe in looking after themselves, and not chasing trouble. If they have a real disagreement with someone, Gypsy or non-Gypsy, they simply move away, and do not return until the trouble is resolved. In a free, nomadic culture it has been possible to do this. Sometimes, a quarrel might be resolved in a fist fight between two men. Whoever is believed by most people to be in the right will probably have more confidence and win the fight; but the loser's honour will be satisfied. Sometimes, the quarrel may become a long-lasting feud, simply because the families' paths do not cross, and grievances may not go away until family friends make an effort to reconcile the feuding parties.

But in the main, Romanichals try to respect each other and avoid conflict. They do not understand why Rom need the *kris*. Why do they pay so much attention to their chiefs (*baré*) when English Gypsies acknowledge no chiefs? Why are the Rom refugees trying so hard to get houses from the Homeless Families Units of local councils, when Romanichals are fighting to live in trailers and not be forced into houses? Nonetheless,

the Gypsy Council has welcomed the Rom refugees, helping them to apply for asylum.

Some Romanichals are worried that the cramped, local authority sites in England may make it harder for Gypsies to avoid trouble. They may stay on a site with neighbours they dislike because of increasing persecution on the road, especially after the Criminal Justice Act of 1994, which gives police and councils powers to move Gypsies on at very short notice. Some fear violence has already become more common. In the USA, by contrast, it is still the easiest thing in the world just to hitch up and go. In Texas, one person in seven lives in a trailer or mobile home anyway, and there is plenty of land.

The feeling that they can move at a moment's notice is precious even to those Romanichals who now live in houses. More than any other Romany group, therefore, the Romanichals have tried to make everything that goes with a travelling lifestyle, the horses and waggons, the trailers, and the trucks, as richly decorated and beautiful as possible.

◀ *At 8 am, with all the ornaments carefully stowed away, an American Romanichal family is setting out from Texas to spend summer in the cooler northern states of the USA.*

Earning a living

People often talk about 'the decline of Gypsy trades', as if without the chance to carve wooden pegs, twist withy baskets and carpet-beaters and tell fortunes, English Gypsy culture would collapse. But the most important Romany traditions of all are adaptation, innovation and flexibility. The most important Gypsy trades are often those that non-Gypsies haven't yet realized are Gypsy trades. As other trades declined after 1945, American Romanichals started 'black-topping' (laying tarmacadam on driveways) and from the 1960s, English Romanichals took up this work, calling it 'tarmacking'.

The Gypsies who spend all of their time working for farmers are the poorest. By 1965, only 15 per cent of Travellers in England and Wales did this, and virtually none in the USA. Farmers do allow Gypsies to stay on their land. But such farmers like to keep control over their workers and are often the first to protest against the building of local authority caravan sites. 'We know who our own good Gypsies are,' said one, 'and if we keep them on our own land, we can be sure of them.' But, when local authority sites are created in rural areas, the Gypsies get the chance to try some scrap-collecting, or landscape-

◄ *Billy-Sam Bryers with his pick-up truck, and tarmac machine, just north of San Antonio, Texas, ready to do a little black-topping.*

gardening, rather than being at the beck and call of the farmer all the time.

More important even than the right to travel is self-employment. Most Romanichals feel that 'to work for a guv'nor' is a '*ladge*'. *Ladge* in Romany means shame or dishonour. Even rural Gypsies who work for one farmer like to present themselves as independent contractors, agreeing to finish a job for an agreed amount, rather than selling their time for a set amount of money a day.

As Gypsies moved into the towns at the end of the nineteenth century they had to find new trades, mainly in scrap-metal collection and other forms of recycling. Their old metal-working skills enabled them to separate, sort and value different metals, and make an instant offer to householders, factory-owners and shop-keepers to turn their rubbish into cash. In 1971, the British Scrap Metal Federation estimated some £200 million was saved each year in foreign exchange through scrap-metal collection. All sorts of other items could also be bought and sold.

▲ *Jim Dunn stands with his great-aunt, Sylvia Dunn, in his dad's scrapyard near Southend. Sylvia, a flower-seller, is also president of the National Association of Gypsy Women.*

Some Gypsies continue to deal in horses and still attend traditional horse-fairs such as Appleby and Stow-in-the-Wold. Other Gypsies deal in cars and trucks, or buy medium-priced antiques and furniture to sell them on profitably for export. In 1965, 52 per cent of all Gypsy men in England called themselves 'general dealers'.

In the twentieth century, men's earnings have become much more important than women's among Romanichals. But most women keep up their earning skills, and try to teach them to their daughters in case they should be needed. Flower-selling is still common. Sylvia Dunn and her daughter,

Donna, run a stall outside a cemetery, where they offer sympathy as well as bouquets. Their customers often come back to thank the Gypsy ladies for giving a word of consolation at the right time.

When Gypsies want to learn a new trade, they go out with friends or relatives who have already mastered it. From the 1960s, tarmacking, roofing and other building-repair skills spread in this way. Romanichals usually only work together as partners, for a share of the profits, and do not employ each other. Some, however, do employ non-Gypsies, often homeless people, whom they call dossers.

In England, most general dealers, tarmackers and roofers can find enough work all year within driving distance of one site. But they still like to go fruit or vegetable picking in the summer. Every year sixty or seventy families camp on a farm in north Essex for two weeks for pea picking. From first light, a long line of men, women and children can be seen sitting cross-legged on the ground, stretched across a vast field, moving slowly forward as nimble fingers pluck the pods from the plants. This is a holiday time, when Gypsies meet friends and family from all over the country.

More specialized traders, such as carpet sellers (one of the oldest Gypsy trades) and antique dealers (often specializing in particular items, such as old radios, or certain ceramics) need to be more mobile to reach a more scattered demand or supply. Two or three families travel the whole country just selling and fitting gates in fields for farmers.

▼ *Percy Harris (Jimmy's dad) helps Bubbles Brazil assemble the goods for her flower stall. Grandmother of several Boxgrove School children, Bubbles is a campaigner for education.*

Specialized trades mean more travelling costs, but Gypsies can make more money from them. The very richest Romanichals, the 2 or 3 per cent who are millionaires, own houses, land and trailers. Some are even property traders. They often keep their Romany background a secret from their business friends. Such rich Romanichals can afford to ignore other Gypsies or non-Gypsies who might condemn them. In recent years, however, it has become easier for educated Romanichals, such as teachers, nurses or lawyers, to be open about being Romany and join with their families in the crowds at Appleby and other fairs. They still may face prejudice, however, from both Gypsies and non-Gypsies.

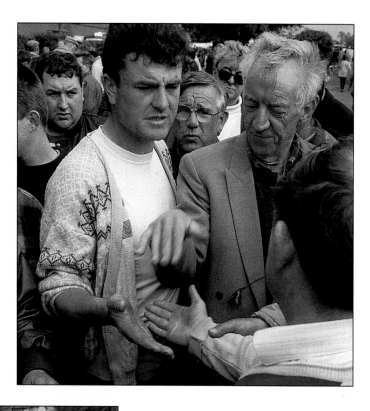

▲ Bargaining for horses at Appleby Fair. The go-between (the man with grey hair) encourages a buyer and seller to 'have a deal!'

◄ Once the two men have clapped their hands on the deal, the go-between is given money 'for a drink' from the pay-out.

 # *Fairs and gatherings*

The great Gypsy fairs didn't begin as Gypsy fairs. They all started as great non-Gypsy gatherings, such as the spring and autumn hiring fairs at Stow-in-the-Wold in Gloucestershire, or Cambridge Midsummer Fair or Appleby Horse Fair in Cumbria. When Gypsies were being persecuted in the sixteenth and seventeenth centuries, groups of families could meet up at these fairs without being noticed because of the great crowds. Nowadays, there are about fifty of these fairs left. Sometimes, the Gypsies are the only people keeping them going, as at Appleby, and Horsemonden in Kent. Non-Gypsy residents, often people who have recently moved to the area, sometimes try to close Gypsy fairs down. Gypsies often have to campaign to protect these fairs.

From the eighteenth century, Gypsies would also gather at large horse-racing meetings, such as Epsom in Surrey or Doncaster in Yorkshire. Recently, big Pentecostal Christian rallies have brought together Gypsies from all round the country.

In the twentieth century, the two largest gatherings are at Epsom Races in the first week of June, followed by Appleby in the second. Many of the better-off Gypsies tow their trailers from one fair to the other.

▼ *Much business is still done at fairs. On the field at Stow Fair, in 1994, a harness is sold from a pick-up truck. Over the fire a kettle prop stands, from which cooking pots can be hung.*

◄ *Fourteen-year-old Billy Robson showing off the paces of a horse he wants to sell at Appleby Fair. He is driving a very light cart of the type used for racing at Appleby. The onlookers stand well clear.*

Epsom Races and Appleby are great occasions. Gypsies meet relatives they have not seen all year. They show off their trailers, and their wooden wagons and flat-carts if they have them. Even the tarmac-rollers on the back of their lorries will be cleaned and polished. The caravan manufacturers show off their latest models, parking them alongside the horse-drawn *vardos*.

Some fairs still serve their original purpose for trading, for both Gypsies and non-Gypsies. Horses are still traded with farmers and non-Gypsy dealers at Appleby, Horsmonden, Stow, and a dozen other fairs – and every week at Southall Market in West London. Strong young men trot the horses bare-back or with flimsy traps down narrow lanes to show them off to potential buyers.

◄ *A quick piece of on-the-spot blacksmithing, shoeing a horse at Appleby Fair.*

Prices are never fixed. Buyers and sellers haggle, encouraged by the crowd around them, until a deal is struck with a sharp clapping of right hands. All the equipment needed for horses will be on sale too – harnesses, saddles and brasses, while blacksmiths bring mobile forges.

Horse trading makes a great tourist attraction, especially at Appleby, where the washing and grooming of horses in the River Eden is often photographed in romantic travel brochures. Gypsies themselves rush to buy published collections of photographs of Appleby – as well as books like the one you are reading now.

Specialist traders come to the fairs, many of them Gypsies themselves. One such man, Charlie Smith, used to commission special plates, cups and saucers from small Staffordshire potteries in the styles Gypsies love. Visiting so many fairs gave him a vision of the Romanichal people as a whole, which he tried to express first by writing articles and poems, and then through voluntary work for the Gypsy Council. Eventually, he was elected as the council's chairman and is now known internationally.

▲ *Charlie Smith with one of his poems. He sold Staffordshire China for years from fair stalls. He still loves beautiful china.*

STRICTLY CASH

They call me the Pot Man.
I travel round the fairs,
Selling fancy china
Pottery and wares.
I'll flash out on a race course
Or down a country lane.
As long as I can deal,
The place is much the same
I stock all the *kubbas*
The Travellers like to buy,
So look upon my stall
And you are sure to buy.
I won't take no cheques
Or fancy plastic trash.
If you want to deal with me,
My terms are strictly cash.

Charlie Smith,
Gypsy Council chairman.

◄ *Luxurious modern trailers at Appleby Fair. Electricity-generators, calor-gas stoves, and a portable satellite dish mean these fairgoers have all the comforts of home.*

Many rural Gypsies prefer to buy their necessities for the year at a fair. Horsemonden Fair in Kent is a tiny fair, held for just one day on a village green, with only about forty stalls. Gypsies do not bring their trailers. But even there young mothers push back prams piled high with fancy cushions, curtains and sheets to their own taste, and children's shoes, while men ponder elastic-sided dealers' boots and ask for tea sets a little more fancy than the one their brothers bought last year. Young people can look for leather jackets and other smart clothes. They also look out for each other. Young Gypsies are allowed to go out if they are accompanied by cousins of the same sex. More than anywhere else, fairs are where Gypsies are likely to meet their future husbands and wives.

▲ *Stow Fair: work over for the day, a group of lads are off on the town. Fairs give them their best opportunity to meet up with other Gypsy young people of their own age.*

Values and religion

▲ *Before the wedding of Lila Burton and John Eves. The bridesmaids pose for the official photographer. Behind them the Gypsies' favourite video man, Bernie Coe, takes informal shots.*

There is no one religion to which all Gypsies belong or ever belonged. But throughout their lives, Romanichals want to do things properly. Marriage is supposed to last a lifetime. Unlike a number of other Gypsy groups who have arranged marriages, young Romanichal women and men choose their own partners. Their parents often try secretly to throw together those they think are suited, but it would be a *bori ladge* (a shame) to say anything publicly. Traditionally, young couples would elope or 'jump the broomstick' (which means to run away across the neighbouring heathlands, often covered in broom) proving that they were old enough to make their own decisions. They would then return to be reconciled with their parents, and, maybe, to have a church wedding.

These pictures are from the wedding of Lila Burton and John Eves. John had proposed and was accepted by Lila and her family without their having to run away. But at the same time they were waiting to hear about one of Lila's brothers, who had eloped in the old-fashioned way a week or two before Lila's wedding. They need not have worried; within a couple of months they had been reconciled with both sets of parents, and preparations were being made for another big wedding.

▲ *Lila has just come back from the hairdresser. She checks her make-up in a wing mirror. Her sister, Mary, waits to help her put on her bridal dress.*

The Romany religious inheritance from India is seen in their cleanliness practices rather than supernatural beliefs, although the Romany words for God *(Devel)* and Devil *(Beng)* are Indian in origin. Cleanliness, and keeping things in their right place, are important to most Romany people across the world. Romanichals show their acceptance of other people by treating them as though they are clean. Allowing others up into your trailer and offering them food or drink is more than just hospitality. If non-Gypsies are visiting Gypsies they should always accept the offer of a cup of tea, because a refusal may be taken as an insult suggesting that those offering it are *mochadi*.

Funerals, too, have to show decent respect for the dead. After a funeral, Gypsies will smash the crockery and burn the trailer and clothes of the person who died, to let their soul depart properly and show they have no need to inherit the belongings of the dead. Parents should give to their children while they are still alive.

Gypsy beliefs about behaviour and relationships are compatible with major European religions such as Islam and Christianity. In the days when most countries had state religions, Gypsies, like the rest of the population, were often forced to go along with these. Books often suggest that this means Gypsies did not really believe in any religion, but this is simply not true. Many Gypsies have been sincere Muslims or Christians, but churches and mosques often did not accept them.

Two English Romanichal Christian preachers were 'Gypsy' Rodney Smith MBE, (1860–1947) and his nephew, G. Bramwell Evens (1884–1943). Bramwell Evens became famous during the 1930s as 'Romany of the BBC', who gave radio talks on wildlife. But Rodney and Bramwell both suffered from prejudice against Gypsies, and from Gypsies who thought they had betrayed their fellow-Gypsies and their ways.

After the wedding

The church ceremony is over. Lila and her mother, Lena, take the first dance at the reception. The difficult parts are all over now and they can relax. Music is provided by the Gypsy rock duo, Spare Parts. In the background many guests are still eating from the lavish buffet laid on at a social club, while Bernie the video man darts around with his camcorder.

For Christianity to become a mass religion among Gypsies, it had to fit in with Gypsy culture. In the last forty years, many Gypsies have become Pentecostals, belonging to a type of Christian church that emphasizes worshipping freely in the holy spirit, with lots of singing, prayers for healing, and 'speaking in tongues'. New members are baptized by being completely submerged in water. Gypsy Pentecostalism started in Brittany in 1952, when two French Gypsies, Mandz and Pounette Duvil, complained to a Pentecostal preacher called Clement LeCossec that if other preachers refused to baptize them, they would baptize each other. Together, they began a Gypsy mission, which now has hundreds of thousands of members in over

▲ *Many Pentecostal Gypsy women cover their heads in church. They do not preach, but they sing and pray loudly.*

forty countries. Roman Catholic and other churches have also started to draw in more Gypsies as worshippers and even as priests.

French Gypsy Pentecostals sent missionaries to England in 1967 and 1975, but had little success until the 1980s, when two men, David Jones and Tom Wilson, were converted. Jones and Wilson are now the leading preachers for several thousand Pentecostal English Romanichals. There are also many Pentecostal Romanichals in the USA. Sometimes, they join with non-Gypsy Pentecostal churches but, as their numbers grow, increasingly they have to start new congregations of their own.

◄ *Gypsy pastor, Jacky Boyd, baptizes Angie Bolesworth. Angie's friend, Josephine Taylor, photographs her commitment to a new life.*

Music, art and culture

Gypsy art reflects Gypsy life. Sometimes in other countries, this is packaged so it can be sold to non-Gypsies by professional musicians and artists, such as Django Reinhardt or The Gypsy Kings in France, Belle Stewart in Scotland or the Furey Brothers in Ireland. But the Romanichals have been much more private. Until recently they have kept their culture and music making to family occasions. They sing and play guitars, accordions, violins and other instruments in their trailers or around outdoor fires, or even in the pub.

Even when English Gypsies are professional musicians, such as Albert Lee the guitarist, or David Essex the singer, the public does not realize that they are actually Romany musicians. David Essex, however, made it very clear in 1995 that his family traditions are still important to him when he opened a new office for the Gypsy Council at Aveley in Essex. 'Gypsy people have been in England for 500 years', he said. 'It is time we had our own place.'

An accordion brings back memories

Alex Smith was born in about 1910. His father sold horses to the Tsar of Russia, and married the daughter of the head kennelman of a Russian Grand Duke. Alex remembers travelling in Russia before the revolution. His family settled in a house when he was a teenager, but he ran away to sea. When he tired of foreign voyages, Alex became a showman with travelling roundabouts, and later took up tarmacking and contracting. He has outlived two wives. Alex now lives on Thurrock Council's Gypsy site. After watching the news on his little television, he turns to the accordion, which can take him back musically to Gypsy folksong, Russian ballads, and fairground and music hall medleys. His store of tunes and stories makes him a living history of the twentieth century.

▲ *Alex plays his accordion at dusk.*

◀ *After Sunday morning church and a large lunch, these American Romanichals sit around to sing and entertain English visitors in the living room of the largest mobile home they have. It has small windows and air-conditioning to keep out the fierce Texas sun. They are singing Gospel songs in a Gypsy style. Pentecostalism has greatly encouraged Romanichal music making.*

Romanichals in England and the USA love Country and Western music. The Pentecostal movement has also brought a gospel influence and has revival meetings, where English Gypsy musicians play and sing. But they also know old English folksongs and their own songs in English Romany, which give us a glimpse of daily life. For example, a verse of a very common Gypsy children's rhyme goes:

'Can you *rokker Romani*?
Can you *fake* the *bosh*?
Can you *dik* the *vesher*,
While *mandi chins* the *cosh*?'

(This means: 'Can you speak Romany? Can you play the violin? Can you watch for the park ranger while I cut some firewood?').

The English Romany dialect is actually a mixture of English and the original Romany. The grammar is mostly taken from English, but the words are a mixture of English and Romany. This makes it very difficult to understand for non-gypsies, and even for other Gypsies who do not speak English. Sometimes it is called the *pogadi jib*. Most Romany dialects in the rest of Europe are not like this. About 5 million people speak Romany with its own grammar and word-endings, which originally came from India. With a little effort, these 5 million can understand each other. Only about half a million speak mixed dialects, such as English Romany. Of this half million, the Romanichals of Britain, the USA and Australia are probably the largest group speaking such a dialect.

Speaking the *pogadi jib* well is one way in which Romanichals show their style to one another. It is very bad manners for anyone under the age of sixty to claim to be good at *rokkering Romani*, but people who do speak well are highly respected. Older men play word-games with each other, making up phrases for new things. For example, American Romanichals have made up the term *shun' n' putch* (meaning 'listen and ask') for the telephone. English Romanichals love this word when they hear it for the first time.

Styles often become popular with Gypsies just when they are going out of fashion with non-Gypsies. For example, English Gypsies took up Beatles' 'mop-top' hairstyles only in the 1970s, flared trousers in the 1980s, and are only just taking up skinhead haircuts in the 1990s! Men often get their best suits made-up by tailors who put in extra pockets and cuff buttons for their Gypsy customers. Gypsy styles are often subtly different. They do not loudly proclaim the wearer to be a Gypsy to someone who does not know Gypsies. But they tell another Gypsy that the wearer knows what is stylish.

Gypsy style is more obvious in what they make for themselves than for others. Wooden pegs, paper flowers, withy baskets and carpet-beaters for sale are sturdily made. But carved peg knives and cane chairs made by older Romanichals for themselves are also works of art.

If they can afford it, Gypsies will spend far more on their plates and saucers, dishes and vases than non-Gypsies. Some American Romanichals buy exquisite ceramics from mainland China. English Romanichals like classic patterns, such as Crown Derby. Buying china is one way of storing their savings, since china can be sold easily to other Gypsies. They also like Staffordshire pieces where they can commission the designs they want, through a dealer such as Charlie Smith, from the potteries.

◄ *This chair was made of woven canes by American Romanichals in the same style as traditional baskets and carpet-beaters.*

▲ *Three decorated vehicles at Appleby Fair: an old Reading wagon, a half-size copy of a bow-top wagon and a restored thirty-five-year-old lorry. Behind is their owner's modern trailer.*

In the 1990s, the recession hit the pottery trade badly but families cherish what they have as a token of good times past. Some modern caravan manufacturers also specialize in Gypsy tastes. They will add chrome and cut glass to windows and walls so that the family buying the trailer can make it unique.

Romanichal Gypsies value tradition as well as style. The beautiful wooden wagons displayed at Appleby Fair keep the old traditions alive, whilst presenting them in a new way. The wooden wagons are decorated more elaborately now than when they were simply functional machines for living in. There are not so many of them about now, however. From the 1950s, there was a decorative gap in Gypsy life. For a while they had their favourite Bedford and Morris trucks painted up. Unfortunately, this made it too easy for the police to know which were the Gypsy vehicles.

So Gypsies turned their hunger to have nice things around them on to a very simple vehicle, the horse-drawn 'flat cart', used for collecting rags or scrap metal. From the 1950s, the Yorkshire Romanichal Jimmy Berry (1908–87), who is now acknowledged as the greatest of all wagon painters, turned the flat cart from a very plain, functional object to a colourful symbol for the general dealer. He, and another Romanichal, Tommy Gaskin, influenced a whole generation of younger Gypsy cart and wagon painters. The result, ironically, was that the wagons often became too costly and beautiful to be used for business.

One Welsh Gypsy wagon restorer, Peter Ingram, has created a museum of Romany life at Selborne in Hampshire. The museum has many examples of old wagons, carts, and decorative art. Another English Gypsy wagon restorer is Tom Lee, who works at his yard in

Stratford, East London. His father and grandfather also built wagons. When they were younger, Peter Ingram and Tom Lee were worried that new laws made it harder for Gypsies to stop by the roadside. They joined a new organization, founded in 1966, called the Gypsy Council, and went to the first World Romany Congress, held near London in 1971, to which Gypsies came from fourteen different countries.

The Gypsy Council fought for caravan sites for Gypsy families and education for Gypsy children. At that time, most schools in England just refused to let Gypsy children attend. The Gypsy Council said that if Gypsy children were to succeed in school, schools would have to respect Romany culture, art, language and music. Tom Lee helped run early caravan school projects in East London, to show ordinary schoolteachers that Gypsy children really did want to learn to read and write. In 1972, Tom formed the Romany Guild.

▶ *In his yard, Tom Lee, now leader of the Romany Guild, is renovating a wagon.*

◀ *This flat cart is just for show. The decoration on the cart is too expensive for the cart to be used for scrap-metal collecting.*

One of the Romany schoolbooks from East London found its way into the hands of a little Hampshire Gypsy girl called Delaine Ayres. Delaine realized she could go to school and still be a Gypsy. At school she could write in her own language as well as in English. She grew up to become a professional artist under her married name, Delaine LeBas. Delaine is just one of several new Gypsy artists who try to express the themes of Gypsy life in the kind of paintings that can be hung on a wall. Two others who also sell paintings are Gill Barron and Norman McDowell.

Better-known, however, are Gypsies who have put their lives into books. Some, such as Fred Wood and Gordon Boswell (father of Gordon Boswell pictured on page 10), have written autobiographies which are easy to find in libraries and have been read by many non-Gypsies. But there are also poets writing especially for other Gypsies. *Poems and Ballads* by Edward Ayres (Midas, 1973) is about everyday life and special events such as fairs and marriages. Julia Gentle's *Tina Lee's Wedding* catches the dream of young love in a Romanichal setting. Margaret Grattan wrote *Paid in Full* when one of her sons had just taken a first-class degree. It expresses her wonder that 'Travelling People such as we, had a son in university' and asserts 'Though his lifestyle may be different, on this you can depend, when speaking of his fore-fathers, he'll say they were Travelling Men'.

Civil rights workers often turn to poetry. Charlie Smith, the chairman of the Gypsy Council (see page 29), and Eli Frankham of the Romany Rights Association (see page 10) have both published books of poems and write about how the 1994 Criminal Justice Act threatens Romany culture in England.

Delaine LeBas

Delaine LeBas comes from a family named Ayres from the New Forest, Hampshire. She went to art school and married fellow-student Damien. Both have exhibited in London and abroad. Damien's family was partly Huguenot (old French Protestants) and partly Irish Traveller – a mixture that took Delaine's Romanichal family some time to accept. She is holding a painting callled *Me and My Husband*. Delaine's vivid, colourful paintings show the same things that Gypsy children paint in schools: trailers, campsites, clothes, the style of travelling life. Her paintings usually have decorative borders with the same patterns as those used by wagon painters.

One important writer for civil rights is Ian Hancock, another of the early Gypsy Council members who attended the 1971 World Romany Congress. Ian was born in London, from a family of Hungarian Gypsies who came to England to work in circuses. Some married English Gypsies and settled in London. When he was thirteen, Ian's parents emigrated to Canada. Ian dropped out of school and returned to London to work with pop musicians. Then, one day, he came across the Creole language of some African musicians, which reminded him of *pogadi jib*. For his own amusement, Ian wrote a dictionary of African Creole. Someone showed it to experts at London University. They could hardly believe it was the work of a school drop-out. He was given a scholarship and within five years he gained a PhD and a job at the University of Texas, USA, where he became one of the world's leading linguists. His book *The Pariah Syndrome* tells the story of centuries of persecution of his own people.

▲ *Professor Ian Hancock is the International Romani Union's delegate to the United Nations. He is wearing a shirt sent to him by English Romanichals to protest against the 1994 Criminal Justice Act.*

◄ *A notice tells Gypsies that the local council has a court order to keep them off this land.*

Working for the future

In the middle of the photo on the back cover Jimmy Harris sits looking at us from the back of a truck. What did the future hold for him when this picture was taken?

Since this picture was taken, Thistlebrook has been rebuilt by Greenwich Council and it looks better. But the council has restricted the keeping of trucks and horses on the site to those who have always kept them there. If Jimmy wants to collect scrap metal when he grows up, he will have to rent a private yard for his lorry. He will have to get a licence to deal with waste materials, and write out a description of every piece of scrap he collects and make three copies. One will go to the person he buys the scrap from, one will go to the scrapyard to which he sells it, and one will be kept for his own records.

Many Gypsies think that new laws threaten the existence of the Gypsy way of life in Britain. The most hated law is the 1994 Criminal Justice Act. People camping by the road or on any land without permission can be arrested and their caravans confiscated. Planning law has also been toughened. The government says caravan sites must no longer be built where they will 'spoil' the countryside, or where they are too far from facilities such as schools or shops, or even where they are too near houses. The 1968 Caravan Sites Act, which said that local councils had to make sites for all Travellers, has been repealed. So although nearly 10,000 families in Britain are on legal council or private sites, about 5,000 families are left with nowhere legal to go.

A Gypsy Council meeting

Charlie Smith chairing a meeting in Peterborough Town Hall of the Gypsy Council for Education, Culture, Welfare and Civil Rights, a leading Gypsy organization. Beside Charlie sits Peter Mercer, the Council's president, who represents the council at international meetings. Peter Mercer is a community worker with Peterborough City Council.

◄ *A Gypsy Education Unit at Appleby Fair. They are giving information on materials used by teachers up and down the country and on the work of Gypsy voluntary organizations.*

In the past, Romanichals reacted to threats in Britain by moving abroad to the USA and Australia, where governments do not restrict travelling. There is more land there and Gypsies can find camping places easily, but there is still prejudice against them. But English Gypsies know that violence and discrimination are even worse in some Eastern European countries. Some have organized lorry-loads of relief for Romanian Gypsies, for whom life is extremely hard. Today, Gypsies from many countries work together to win fair treatment, and the chance to learn to read and write, and secure places to live for Gypsies everywhere. Leaders such as Ian Hancock, Peter Mercer, and a brilliant Romanian Romany intellectual called Nicolae Gheorghe, work through the International Romani Union to make the United Nations and the European Community realize that Romany peoples deserve a better future.

► *Setting up a deal at Appleby Fair. Gypsy business must move with the times and the mobile phone is one modern invention that can help preserve a threatened culture.*

Timeline

◄ *A meeting of the International Romani Union in Brno, Czech Republic.*

Important Dates in Gypsy History:

Around 1000	Romany people reach the area of modern Turkey and Greece.
1505	First record of Gypsies in Britain.
1530	First law expelling Gypsies from England.
1554	First law making being an immigrant Gypsy in England a crime punishable by death.
1596	106 men and women condemned to death at York just for being Gypsies, but only 9 are executed. The others prove they were born in England.
1650s	Last known execution for being Gypsies, in Suffolk. Others are transported to America.
1660–1800	The identity of the English Gypsy Romanichal group has been formed. They survive by working for local people who know them.
1811	Trinity Cooper, a Gypsy girl aged thirteen, demands to be let into a charity school for 'ragged children' in Clapham, near London, with her two brothers. They are finally admitted.
1816	John Hoyland, a Quaker, writes the first serious book calling for better treatment for Gypsies in England. Several charitable projects follow; but many Gypsies are transported as criminals to Australia.
1830s	First wooden horse-drawn caravans developed.
1880s	Agricultural depression brings poverty to many Gypsies, who move to squatter areas near towns.
1885–95	Unsuccessful attempts to introduce Moveable Dwellings Bills in Parliament to regulate Gypsy life.
1889	The Showmen's Guild formed to oppose Moveable Dwellings Bills: Showmen begin to become a distinct group from other Travellers or Gypsies.
1908	Children's Act: Education made compulsory for Travelling Gypsy children, but only for half the year. This was continued in the 1944 Education Act, but many Gypsy children still have no schooling.

▲ *This young boy is looking after his dad's horse at Appleby Fair.*

Important Dates in Gypsy History:	
1939–45	Second World War. Up to 500,000 Gypsies killed in Europe; Nazis draw up lists of English Gypsies for internment. British government creates caravan sites for families of Gypsies in the army or doing farm labour. These sites are closed after the war.
1945–60	Gypsies begin to use motor-drawn trailers, and buy land for their own stopping-places.
1960	Caravan Sites (Control of Development) Act stops new private sites being built until 1972. Eviction and harassment of Gypsies starts to reach a crisis.
1966	Growing eviction and harassment leads to formation of Gypsy Council to fight for sites.
1967	First Gypsy Council summer school, in Essex. National Gypsy Education Council follows in 1970 (renamed Gypsy Council for Education, Culture, Welfare and Civil Rights in 1991).
1968	Caravan Sites Act insists that from 1970, local authorities should provide caravan sites for Gypsies. This Act is never fully enforced.
1971	First World Romany Congress held in London.
1972	Government begins to exempt some councils from building sites. The Gypsy Council begins to split. Government starts to give grants only to Gypsy organizations who co-operate with it.
1978	Second World Romany Congress in Switzerland, founds International Romani Union – accepted as representing Gypsies by the United Nations in 1979.
1989	22 May: European Union starts five-year programme for the education of Gypsy children.
1994	Criminal Justice Act abolishes Caravan Sites Act leaving about 5,000 families with no legal home. British Gypsies look to Europe for protection.

Glossary

Gypsy words

Bokkali Hungry.
Cant The three languages of the Scottish Travellers.
Chins Cuts.
Cosh Stick.
Devel God.
Dik See, watch for.
Fake the bosh Play the violin.
Gammon The language of the Irish Travellers.
Gaujos Non-Gypsies.
Jib Tongue, language.
Kalderash Coppersmiths – a widespread. group of East European Rom.
Kalé (**Feminine Kali**), **Calé, Kaale** Welsh, Spanish and Finnish Gypsies.
Kris Tribunal or trial among some East European Rom.
Kubbas Things.
Ladge, Ladged Shame, ashamed.
Lolli Red.
Mandi I, me.
Minceir Irish Travellers (in *Gammon*).
Mochadi Unclean, polluted, filthy.
Nawkens Scottish Travellers (in *Cant*).
Pobbel Apple.
Pogadi Broken.
Prastering Saster Bicycle.
Rokker Speak.
Rom (1) In English Romany, (a) husband (b) foreign Gypsy (2) In East European Romany, a Gypsy.
Romani (adjective) Romany, Gypsy.
Romanichals (noun) English Gypsy.
Shun 'n' putch Telephone.
Sinti German Gypsies.
Vardos Wooden, horse-drawn caravans.
Vesher Park ranger, gamekeeper.

Difficult English words

Ancestors People in a person's family who are no longer alive.
Asphalt A tarry surface used on roads.
Asylum A place of safety or refuge.
Broom A prickly plant with small yellow flowers.
Civil rights The entitlements of a citizen.
Conscripted When a person is called up to serve in the armed forces.
Contractors People who agree to work or supply goods for a set amount of money.
Forge A fireplace used by metalsmiths.
General dealers Traders who will carry out many different kinds of work.
Internment Imprisonment without trial.
Latrines Communal lavatories in camps or barracks.
Medleys Mixtures of different song.
Missionaries People sent to another country on a religious mission.
Nobility People of high, social rank.
Pentecostal A form of Christianity which emphasizes the Holy Spirit.
Persecutions When a group of people is harassed or hunted down.
Prejudiced To have an unfair opinion or feeling about someone or something.
Recession A temporary decline in economic activity or prosperity in a country.
Refugees People fleeing from war or persecution who seek shelter in another country.
Repealed When a law is abolished.
Traps Small, two-wheeled, open, horse-drawn carriages.
Vagrants People who have no settled home.
Withy A reed or stalk that is used to make woven baskets.

Further information

Books to read

For younger readers
The Life and Story of May Orchard, Dorothy Orchard, (Devon Traveller Education Service, 1995)
Moving with the Times, Goodiy Reilly, (Devon Traveller Education Service, 1995)
Poems by Eli, Eli Frankham (Private, 1991)
Not all Wagons and Lanes, Charles Smith, (G.C.E.C.W.C.R./Essex Traveller Education Service, 1995)

For older readers and reference
Dictionary of the English Romani Dialect – Romani Rokkeripen To-Divvus, Ed. Thomas Acton and Donald Kenrick, (Romanestan Publications, 1985). The most recent study of *pogadi jib*.
The Gypsies, Angus Fraser, (Blackwell, 1992)
On the Verge – The Gypsies of England, D. Kenrick and S. Bakewell, (University of Hertfordshire Press 2nd ed., 1995)
Roma/Gypsies: A European Minority, Nicolae Gheorghe and Jean-Pierre Liégois, (Minority Rights Group International, 1995)
The Pariah Syndrome, Ian F. Hancock, (Karoma, 1988)

Useful addresses

Romanichal Gypsy Organizations
Gypsy Council for Education, Culture, Welfare and Civil Rights, 8 Hall Road, Aveley, Essex, RM15 4HD
Romany Guild, 62 Temple Mills Lane, London E15
National Association of Gypsy Women, Meadowview, Goldsmith Drive, Lower Holbridge Road, Rayleigh, Essex
National Romany Rights Association, Roman Bank, Walpole St Andrew, Cambs.

Other organizations concerned with Gypsies
Advisory Council for the Education of Romanies and Other Travellers, Moot House, The Stow, Harlow, Essex CM20 3AG

National Association of Teachers of Travellers, The Graisely Centre, Pool Street, Wolverhampton WV2 4NE

Museums
The Romany Folklore Museum, Limes End Yard, High Street, Selborne, Nr. Alton, Hants GU34 3JW
Tel: 01420 511480

Wheelwrights Working Museum and Gypsy Folklore Collection, Webbington Loxton, Nr. Axbridge, Somerset BS26 2HX
Tel: 01934 750841

The Gordon Boswell Romany Museum, Clay Lane, Spalding, Lincs. PE12 6BC
Tel: 01775 710599

Index

Numbers in **bold** refer to pictures as well as text.